Little Talks with Jesus

Rhyming Prayers For Everyday Use!

Index

Index

Day Starter

Whether I study, work, or play,
You're out front to lead the way.
Help me stay close and do as You tell.
You're my big brother who guides me well.

"Trust in the Lord with all your heart; and lean not to your own understanding. In all your ways acknowledge Him, and He shall direct your paths" (Proverbs 3:5–6 AKJV).

School Time

"I can do everything through Christ, who gives me strength" (Philippians 4:13 NLT).

So many skills in life to gain,
And knowledge to expand.
Please help my teachers well explain,
And for me to understand.

Appreciation

Some drive the buses
Others sew our clothes.
Some bag our groceries
Or sell shoes to cover toes.

Make me a blessing when I meet
Those who care for others' needs.
Help me show appreciation,
Returning kindness for their deeds.

School Bus

"Love your neighbor as yourself" (Matthew 19:19 AKJV).

Appreciation

Thank You for the farmers
Who grow food and work the soil.
Please bless both them and others
Who with the livestock toil.

And take care of the fishermen
Who feed us from the sea,
And the dairymen and everyone
Who provide food for all, plus me.

Eggs

Vegetables

"The Lord is my shepherd, I shall not want" (Psalm 23:1 KJV).

Caring for Others

Jesus, please keep the younger kids safe.

Help me to do my best for others,
By remembering them in prayer.
Telling You about their needs,
Is the greatest type of care.

School

"Pray for all people. Ask God to help them" (1 Timothy 2:1 NLT).

Thank You for this pet of mine
That means so much to me.
Please guide me in my care of him,
So he's healthy and worry-free.

"The godly care for their animals" (Proverbs 12:10 NLT).

Pets

I have a little pet
You've entrusted to my care.
Help me treat her as I should.
This is my earnest prayer.

"A person who is faithful
in small things will be
faithful with much"
(Luke 16:10, *paraphrased*).

Octopus
Food

Our World

I'm only one small person
Within this world so grand.
Please help me to do my
  part
To preserve it as I can.

I know it's no small task
To care for air, water, and land.
But You can use my small ways
To make a difference where I
  can.

"The whole earth is full of God's glory"
(Isaiah 6:3, *paraphrased*).

Such a beautiful world You've created:
Plants and animals both big and small,
Tiny ants that dig in the garden,
And giraffes that grow so tall.

In the midst of all this beauty,
You made one such as me.
Help me show my appreciation
By caring for all I see.

"The earth is the Lord's, and all that is in it"
(Psalm 24:1, *paraphrased*).

Patience

Sometimes I lack patience
Waiting for a special day.
Help me notice the good things
To enjoy along the way.

"Make the most of every opportunity"
(Ephesians 5:16 NLT).

Patience

When I am in a hurry
To complete a difficult task,
Please help me work with patience,
So in "well done" I'll bask.

"The hand of the diligent brings success" (Proverbs 10:4, *paraphrased*).

Jesus, You've given me so much,
Help me give back to You
By being for others a loving touch
With kind deeds that I do.

"Be kind to each other, tenderhearted, forgiving one another, just as God through Christ has forgiven you"
(Ephesians 4:32 NLT).

"In every thing give thanks:
for this is the will of God in
Christ Jesus concerning you"
(1 Thessalonians 5:18 AKJV).

I'm happy for the food You give,
And thank You for Your care.
Please bless the one who cooked this meal,
This is my sincere prayer.

Bedtime

Off to bed I go tonight.
Even in the dark, You are my light.
Diligently cared for within Your sight.
Thank You for how You hold me tight.

"I will lie down in peace to sleep, because
You, Lord, keep me safe" (Psalm 4:8, *paraphrased*).

Communicating with God

Whenever I look to You in praise
Or read Your words to connect,
I always cherish my time with You—
Time on Your grace to reflect.

"In the beginning was the Word, and the Word was with God, and the Word was God" (John 1:1 KJV).

Communicating with God

When talking with You in prayer,
Or listening to Your voice through Your Word,
Please focus my attention on You,
So the marvels You speak of are heard!

"The entrance of Your words gives light;
it gives understanding" (Psalm 119:130 AKJV).

Angels

You promise that Your angels
Will surround me with Your care.
They'll eagerly protect me,
Even when I'm unaware.

Please help me do my part
By staying close to You,
Praising You, and obeying
Your guidance in all I do.

"He will order his angels to protect you" (Psalm 91:11 NLT).

Angels

During trying times,
When I'm anxious or afraid,
Thank You for being eager
To send angels to my aid.

"I send an angel before you to care for you"
(Exodus 23:20, *paraphrased*).

Respect

To say please and thank you,
To answer another and not neglect,
To listen well and not interrupt,
Shows others my respect.

To be considerate of another's view,
To clean up after a project,
To hold the door for another to pass,
Shows others my respect.

In the things that You do,
You show others great respect.
Please help me follow Your example,
And show others my respect.

"In honor, prefer one another"
(Romans 12:10, *paraphrased*).

Respect

I want to prefer others to myself
And treat them with respect.
Help me consider them like You do;
Your caring ways to reflect.

"Treat others as you would like them to treat you"
(Luke 6:31, *paraphrased*).

It's fun to be with others
Who enjoy the things I do.
We have our common interests
That give us a special glue.

Please help me to be friendly
When another comes along
Who presents another interest
But still wants to belong.

"For a person to have friends, he must be friendly"
(Proverbs 18:24, *paraphrased*).

Understanding Others

I know that when I'm open,
To hear another's view,
I can learn from their opinion
Even when it's something new.
I want to be considerate
Of another's thought or finding.
I ask You for acceptance
And to be more understanding.

"Be swift to hear, slow to speak, slow to anger"
(James 1:19, paraphrased).

Sportsmanship

Thank You for the games we play,
And for good times together.
Help us to play fair and well
And show concern for one another.

"In honor, prefer one another" (Romans 12:10, *paraphrased*).

Though I'm eager to play this game,
It bothers me if I lose.
I pray to focus on the fun;
Enjoyment is what I choose.

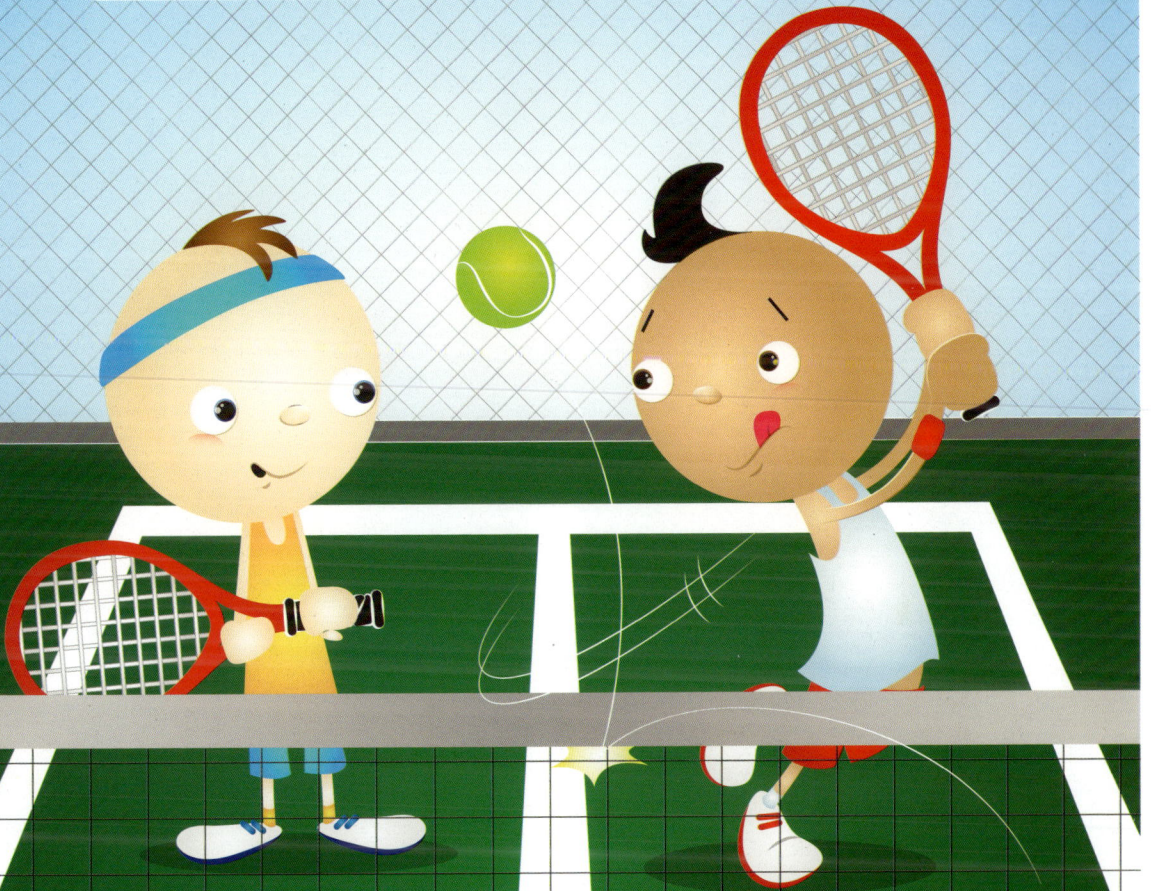

Whatsoever things are true, honest, just, pure, lovely, and of good report; think on these things (Philippians 4:8, *paraphrased*).

Agreeable or Quarrelsome?

I argued with my brother,
Then I argued with my friend.
Help me care more for others,
Make understanding my new trend.

"Search for ways to make peace and to help others"
(Romans 14:19, *paraphrased*).

Agreeable or Quarrelsome?

If I push to have my own way,
It can make another sad.
Teach me to think of others' needs
And how to make them glad.

03:01

"Don't only look out for your own good, but look for ways to help others" (Philippians 2:4, *paraphrased*).

Forgiveness

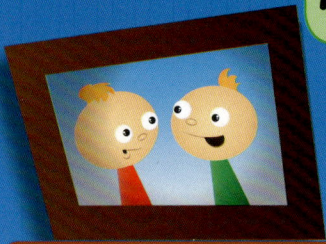

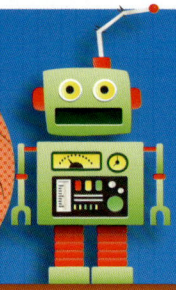

Dear Jesus,
Help me be like You,
Forgiving others
As You forgive me too.

"Remember, the Lord forgave you, so you must forgive others" (Colossians 3:13 NLT).

Forgiveness

Even if another brings me down
With an unkind word and deed,
Help Your smile replace my frown,
To lift others who are in need.

"Love those who are unfriendly to you.
Do good to those who harass you" (Luke 6:27, *paraphrased*).

Do What's Right

I want to follow closely
And do what You teach is best.
Please help me to choose rightly,
No matter what the test.

"If you love me, keep my commandments" (John 14:15 AKJV).

Challenges

I'm facing another challenge,
While learning something new.
I pray for You to help me
Not give up but see it through.

"Be diligent in what you
do and you will prosper"
(Proverbs 13:4, *paraphrased*).

Courage

When I'm afraid, what I must do
Is call Your name and trust in You.
You'll take my hand and lead me on.
I'm safe with You, for You are strong.

"The Lord is my helper, and I will not fear" (Hebrews 13:6 AKJV).

When I worry about "What if?"
I can bring my fears to You.
You remind me of Your faithful care
To overcome; You see me through.

"You will keep in perfect peace all who trust in you"
(Isaiah 26:3 NLT).

Generosity

Giving to another
Often encourages two:
The one who is the receiver
And me the giver, too.

Help me consider another's joy
And not just think of mine.
Then I can join in giving
And bring to each
face a shine.

"Give, and it will be given to you"
(Luke 6:38, *paraphrased*).

Generosity

If I can make someone happy
By lending a helping hand,
Please help me do what's needed,
While setting aside my plan.

"Freely you have received, freely give" (Matthew 10:8 AKJV).

Encouragement

To offer a friend encouragement
Gives them a personal lift.
Please remind me to support others
With this strengthening gift.

YOU CAN DO it

"Let's give others encouragement"
(Romans 14:19, *paraphrased*).

Encouragement

Teach me to bring out the best in friends,
Encouraging their skills to grow.
Show me times to offer this boost,
Helping Your love through me to flow.

"Encourage each other and build each other up"
(1 Thessalonians 5:11 NLT).

Birthday

You created me so wonderfully.
I am blessed, so help me be
A channel of Your love through me,
Kindheartedness for all to see.

"I am wonderfully made" (Psalm 139:14, *paraphrased*).

Friends and Loved Ones

Thank You for friends and family,
Who fill my days with cheer.
Please watch over and care for them,
And to Your heart keep them near.

"When I pray for you, I pray with joy"
(Philippians 1:4, *paraphrased*).

Saying Goodbye

The fun friends that I have
Are a wonderful gift.
I've enjoyed being with them.
My life they do lift.

Now it's time to say goodbye,
So I'll send them on their way
With words of love and prayers
For joy-filled lives each coming day.

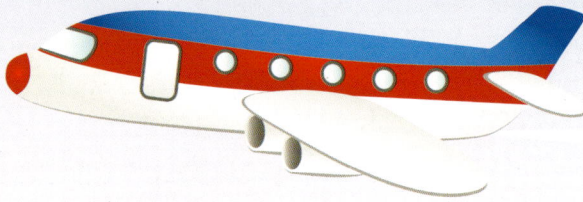

"I wish for good things for you"
(3 John 2, *paraphrased*).

Now our loved one has departed.
With trust we give her back to You,
We're thankful for the time we had,
For love between us that will stay true.

"I'm convinced that neither death, nor life, nor spiritual beings, nor rulers, nor powers, nor worries, nor any creature, will be able to separate us from the love of God in Christ Jesus our Lord"
(Romans 8:38-39, paraphrased).

Our New Family Member

Our family is blessed with a baby,
Who needs extra love and tender care.
Please help us to make baby happy;
I ask this of You in my prayer.

"Children are a gift from God" (Psalm 127:3, *paraphrased*).

There's someone new in our family,
You sent as a wonderful treat!
Each person is a gift of Your love;
And makes all of our lives more
    complete.

*"Every good gift, and every perfect gift is from above,
and comes down from the Father of lights"* (James 1:17 AKJV).

Grandparents

Grandma likes to make me glad.
Help me make her happy, too,
I wish to help and listen well,
To flow with what she plans to do.

"Grandchildren are the crown of the elderly" (Proverbs 17:6, paraphased).

45

Grandparents

Help me respect and make Granddad glad,
Whether he's thoughtful or acts like a clown.
My granddad is always such a treat;
A special person to have around.

"A merry heart does good like a medicine"
(Proverbs 17:22 AKJV).

Christmas

On this special day of Christmas,
My heart is full of joy.
I'm amazed You lived in our world,
As a baby and a boy.

I know You can relate to me,
And all children on this earth.
Now for this I praise You,
As I celebrate Your birth!

"To us a child is born, to us a son is given" (Isaiah 9:6 AKJV).

Let Your gladness fill my heart,
Whether my experience is sweet or tart.
A joyful smile will brighten my day,
And Your strength will better my way.

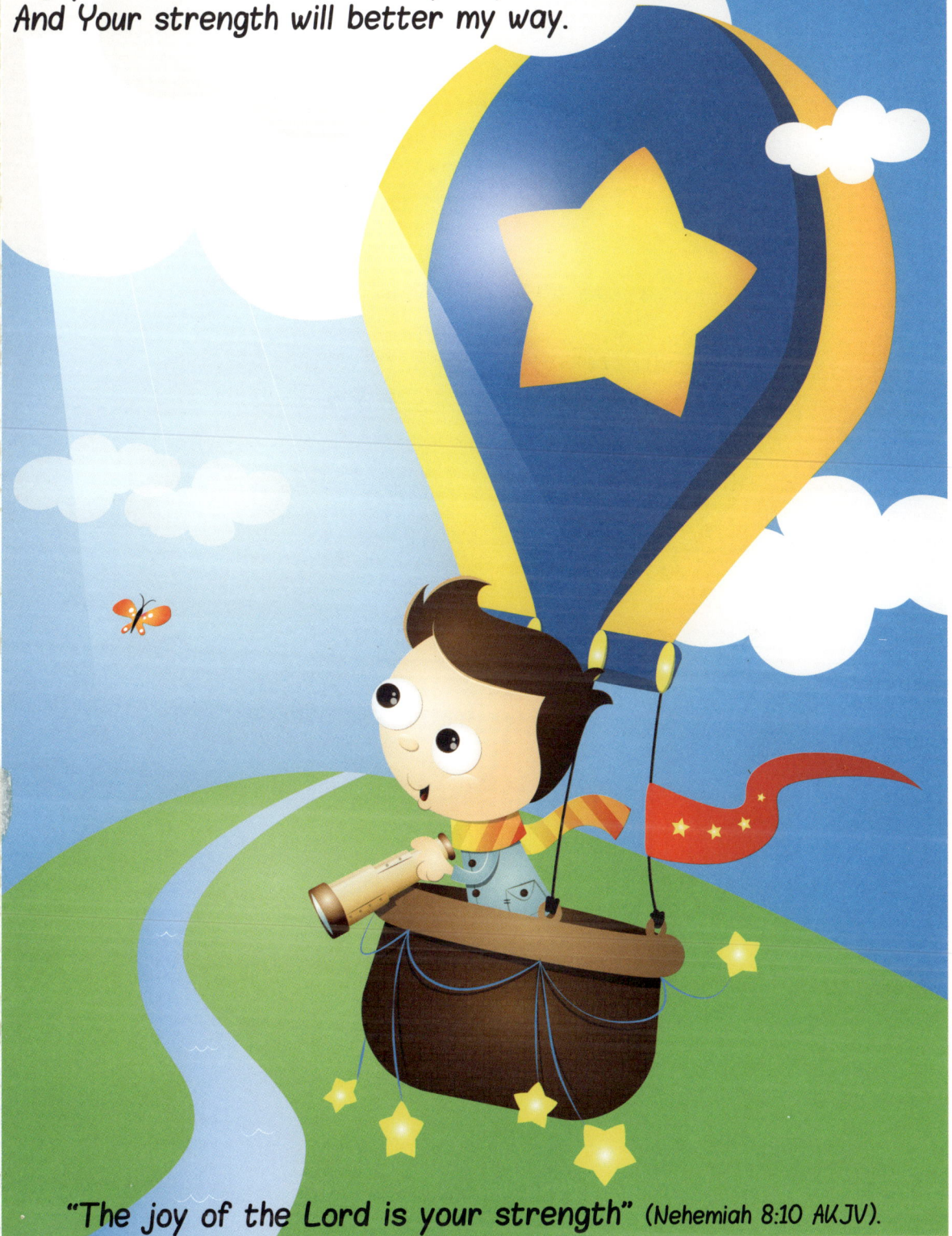

"The joy of the Lord is your strength" (Nehemiah 8:10 AKJV).